This Notebook Belongs To:

....

Date:

....

www.ingramcontent.com/pod-product-compliance
Lightning Source LLC
Chambersburg PA
CBHW052037280526
45791CB00010B/2987